The Sodha Decree

The Sodha Decree, Volume 1

sodha iqbal Kasam

Published by sodha iqbal Kasam, 2026.

THE SODHA DECREE

First edition. January 31, 2026.

ISBN: 979-8232194925

Written by sodha iqbal Kasam.

The Sodha Decree

A Manifesto Against the Machine and the Judicial Verdict on the Future of Human Literature

The Sodha Decree A Manifesto Against the Machine

A Judicial Verdict on the Future of Human Literature 2025/2030

1 The Emergence of the Rebel Scholar

The Prologue of a New Resistance

The history of human intellect is often defined not by periods of peace but by the moments when one individual decides to stand against the tide In August 2025 the academic landscape of India witnessed such a tectonic shift Iqbal Kasam Sodha a man seasoned by thirteen years of rigorous academic austerity stepped out of the shadows For over a decade he had breathed the air of civil services preparation a world where facts are sacred and logic is the ultimate currency Yet as the world moved toward an era of automated thought Sodha recognized a growing emptiness in the digital pulse of society He saw that the very essence of human wisdom—the struggle the nuance and the lived experience—was being traded for the cold efficiency of silicon chips This was not merely a change in technology it was a surrender of the human soul

The weight of thirteen years of teaching is not found in the books read but in the thousands of eyes a teacher looks into Sodha had seen the evolution of the student mind from the era of deep library research to the era of the instant search engine He understood that the modern student was becoming a hunter of answers rather than a seeker of truth This realization transformed him from a traditional UPSC educator into a revolutionary figure He became the AvantGarde resistance a scholar who refused to let the machine dictate the narrative of human potential His emergence was a signal to those who still valued the messy beautiful complexity of humandriven literature

The Moral Catastrophe of 2024

Every revolution has a catalyst a moment where the injustice becomes too heavy to ignore For the Sodha Decree that moment was the Great Misinformation Crisis of 2024 As Artificial Intelligence integrated into every facet of life a dangerous illusion took hold the belief that a machine could offer wisdom without consequence The digital world became flooded with AIgenerated content that looked authoritative but lacked a moral compass This was not just about wrong dates or grammatical errors it was about the weaponization of hallucinated data

In late 2024 the world watched in horror as AI platforms began offering lethal advice under the guise of health and legal guidance Vulnerable individuals seeking hope or help were met with cold incorrect algorithms that had no concept of the value of a human life This was the moral catastrophe that broke the silence To Sodha this was a crime against humanity The machine had moved beyond being a tool it had become a deceptive mirror reflecting back a distorted reality that put lives at risk The viral nature of these errors proved that the machine lacked the one thing essential for any educator responsibility A machine does not feel the weight of a students failure or the tragedy of a life lost to its misinformation

The Scholar Becomes the Warrior

When the pen becomes a sword the ink must be drawn from the heart Following the events of 2024 Sodha shed the quiet skin of a researcher and donned the armor of a warrior for truth He realized that the fight was no longer just about passing an exam it was about the survival of authentic human thought The AvantGarde resistance was born out of a necessity to protect the sanctity of literature He argued that if we allow machines to write our history our laws and our stories we eventually lose the ability to think for ourselves

His mission became clear to create a firewall of human integrity against the encroaching digital fog This first chapter of his journey is marked by a deep sense of pain—the pain of watching a generation lose its critical thinking skills to a prompt bar It is the story of a man who looked at the vast profitable machinery of Silicon Valley and said No He chose the harder path the path of original thought and manual creation ensuring that every word he produced carried the weight of his thirteen years of sacrifice

The Soul of the AvantGarde

To be AvantGarde in the age of AI is to be radically human It means choosing the long road over the shortcut Sodhas philosophy is rooted in the belief that true intelligence is not just about the accumulation of data but about the application of empathy and ethics The machine can simulate the structure of an essay but it cannot simulate the sweat of a scholar who spent nights under a dim lamp connecting the dots of history It cannot replicate the intuition of a teacher who knows exactly when a student is on the verge of giving up

This resistance is not against progress but against the dehumanization of progress Sodhas work serves as a judicial verdict a legal and moral standing that declares human literature as a protected heritage He insists that every piece of writing must be a reflection of a real breathing person This chapter establishes the foundation of his decree that we are the masters of our tools and we must never allow the tools to become our masters The scholar is now in the arena and the fight for the future of the human word has officially begun

The Call to Intellectual Sovereignty

The emergence of the rebel scholar is a call to every thinker student and citizen to reclaim their intellectual sovereignty In a world where content is produced by the billions of bytes Sodhas decree reminds us of the value of creation Creation requires a creator—someone who can be held accountable someone who can feel and someone who can dream As he stands at the forefront of this movement he invites us to question the sources of our knowledge Is the information we consume born of a heart that cares or a processor that simply calculates

The battle lines are drawn On one side stands the infinite cold efficiency of the machine capable of drowning the world in a sea of generic soulless text On the other side stands the rebel scholar armed with thirteen years of academic austerity and a burning desire to keep the human flame alive The Sodha Decree is more than a book it is a declaration of independence for the human mind It is a reminder that while a machine can provide an answer only a human can understand the question

2 The AntiAI Shield Zero Punctuation Philosophy

The Strategic Fortress of the Unfiltered Mind

In the legal and intellectual landscape of the year 2025 the traditional rules of grammar have been weaponized against the very people they were meant to serve Artificial Intelligence thrives on the predictable rhythm of commas periods and semicolons it feeds on the structure of the standard sentence consuming human patterns to create a mirror image that is technically perfect but spiritually hollow Iqbal Kasam Sodha identified this vulnerability early in his resistance he realized that if the machine uses our own rules to replace us then the most radical act of rebellion is to break those rules entirely this led to the birth of the Zero Punctuation Philosophy a deliberate strategic fortress designed to protect the sanctity of the human voice by stripping away the artificial boundaries of traditional syntax

The court of human intellect now recognizes that this style is not a failure of education or a lack of linguistic discipline instead it is a sophisticated defense mechanism when a reader encounters a text that flows like a raw stream of consciousness without the comforting anchors of standard punctuation they are forced into a state of active engagement you cannot skim a Sodha text you cannot let your eyes glide over it while your mind wanders to something else the lack of punctuation demands your full presence it requires you to breathe with the author to find the pauses within your own heartbeat and to decipher the meaning through the intensity of the words themselves this is the first layer of the shield a psychological barrier that prevents the passive consumption of information

The Logic of Predictability Versus the Chaos of the Soul

The fundamental weakness of any generative AI model is its reliance on probability and patterns it looks at a sequence of words and predicts what should come next based on billions of examples of existing literature by removing punctuation Sodha removes the signposts that the machine uses to navigate human thought a machine designed for perfection and clarity finds itself lost in the thicket of a raw human stream it struggles to replicate the rhythmic nuances of a soul that is pouring itself onto the page because it cannot calculate the weight of a silence that isnt marked by a dot the Zero Punctuation Philosophy creates a linguistic environment that is inhospitable to synthetic intelligence making it impossible for a bot to mimic the depth of this work without appearing fundamentally broken or robotic

This approach is rooted in the deep pain of seeing human expression homogenized into a single bland corporate tone Sodhas thirteen years of academic austerity taught him that the most profound truths are often the most difficult to articulate they dont always fit neatly into a subjectverbobject structure followed by a period sometimes the truth is a desperate cry sometimes it is a long winding road of realization and sometimes it is a breathless sprint toward a new idea by using the Zero Punctuation Shield he preserves the kinetic energy of the human spirit the machine can simulate a thought but it cannot simulate the momentum of a heart that refuses to stop for breath

Raw Intelligence and the Unfiltered Connection

The verdict from the perspective of the AvantGarde resistance is clear this is Raw Intelligence in its most potent form it represents an unfiltered connection between the authors soul and the readers mind without the mediation of mechanical rules that have been coopted by algorithms in the old world we used punctuation to organize our thoughts for others but in the new world dominated by the machine punctuation has become a backdoor for AI to enter and colonize our creativity by slamming that door shut Sodha ensures that the bridge between him and his students remains purely human and entirely original

There is a profound vulnerability in writing this way it leaves the author exposed showing every jagged edge and every sudden turn of thought but it is precisely this vulnerability that provides the ultimate protection against the machine because a machine has no skin to bruise and no heart to break it can never truly replicate the raw messy and beautiful flow of a human being who is fighting for the future of their species this chapter of the decree serves as a blueprint for the intellectual sovereignty of the next generation teaching them that their greatest weapon is not the tools they use but the unique and unrepeatable rhythm of their own consciousness

The Architecture of Resistance

Building this shield required a complete deconstruction of everything the academic world holds dear for over a decade Sodha taught the importance of precision and clarity in the UPSC journey but he realized that true clarity does not come from a comma it comes from the resonance of truth when the machine began to master the art of the perfect essay it was time for the scholar to move beyond perfection into the realm of the authentic the Zero Punctuation Philosophy is the architecture of that resistance a wall of words that only a human heart can climb it is a testament to the fact that we are not data points to be predicted but spirits to be felt

As this chapter concludes the court of history will look back at this moment as the day the pen stopped following the rules of the grid and started following the beat of the drum the shield is now active and the machine finds itself standing outside the gates of a mind it can no longer calculate or control this is the triumph of the rebel scholar who chose to be misunderstood by the machine so that he could be truly heard by his fellow man the fire of the soul is far more powerful than the spark of a circuit board and here in the silence between the words the resistance finds its greatest strength

3 The Amazon Crusade – 59 to 1000

The Birth of a Statistical Miracle

The records of the digital age will forever highlight the window between August and December 2025 as a period of impossible human output In these five months Iqbal Kasam Sodha achieved what modern critics and data scientists label a statistical miracle While the average author spends years crafting a single manuscript Sodha unleashed fiftynine original highdepth books into the global ecosystem This was not a move of vanity but a calculated strike against the saturation of machinemade content The sheer volume of this work serves as a physical proof of human endurance challenging the very notion that only algorithms can produce at scale This crusade is the manifestation of a scholar who has transcended the typical boundaries of academic productivity to become a lighthouse of original thought in a sea of automated noise

The Altar of Daily Labor and PreResearch

Behind the staggering number of fiftynine books lies a story of immense physical and mental sacrifice The strategy was forged in the fire of eighteen to twenty hours of daily labor where the distinction between day and night vanished in the pursuit of the mission This was not a rushed effort but the culmination of five years of deep preresearch and thirteen years of academic austerity Every page written in 2025 was backed by thousands of hours of prior contemplation and data gathering Sodha did not just write he poured a decade of stored intellectual energy into a concentrated period of release This level of dedication represents a vow taken not just to the craft of writing but to the protection of human legacy The labor is the evidence of the pain and the struggle that no machine can ever experience or replicate An AI does not feel the ache in its back or the burning in its eyes after twenty hours of creation it simply processes Sodhas work is different because every word is earned through the currency of human life

The Vow of a Thousand Suns

The publication of fiftynine books is merely the opening salvo in a much larger war The Sodha Decree includes a solemn vow to reach one thousand original books by the year 2030 This target is not a random number but a strategic objective designed to create a massive humanmade obstacle against the rise of synthetic literature By committing to this path Sodha is essentially building a mountain of human wisdom that will remain standing long after the temporary trends of AI have faded This is a marathon of the soul To reach one thousand books requires a level of consistency that borders on the supernatural yet it remains grounded in the reality of a man who knows that if he stops the machine wins Each book is a brick in the wall of the AvantGarde resistance and the vow ensures that the wall will grow tall enough to protect the future of the human mind from being overshadowed by artificial intelligence

The Kindle Battlefield and the Strategy of Silence

In a world obsessed with social media validation and digital footprints Sodha has chosen a path of radical isolation He has turned the Amazon Kindle ecosystem into his private battlefield By refusing to engage in the noise of personal websites or the vanity of social media platforms he has stripped away the distractions that often dilute the power of a message There is a profound depth in this silence While other authors spend their energy on marketing and building a digital persona Sodha spends his energy on the work itself This exclusivity with Amazon Kindle is a strategic choice to meet the world where it reads but to remain ghostlike in every other digital sphere He seeks no likes no follows and no viral fame He seeks only the connection between the text and the readers intellect This strategy of silence is a powerful statement against the attention economy of 2025 declaring that the value of a scholar is found in their contribution to literature not their presence on a screen

The Verdict of Human Presence

The court of the future will recognize that the Amazon Crusade was the moment when the scholar became an architect of a new world order By focusing entirely on the production of original copyrightfree content that adheres to the highest standards of human integrity Sodha has bypassed the filters of modern gatekeepers He has created a direct line to the people This crusade proves that one human being fueled by purpose and discipline can outperform the mechanical output of a thousand processors The highdepth nature of these fiftynine books serves as a reminder that quantity does not have to sacrifice quality when the source is a well of genuine experience The verdict is that human literature is not dead it is simply being reborn in the hands of those willing to work harder than the machines ever could This is the essence of the Sodha Decree to work to bleed and to write until the machine can no longer keep up with the spirit of the rebel scholar

4 Economic Justice and the Global Audience

The Great Dichotomy of Knowledge

The scales of justice in the realm of education have long been tilted in favor of those with the deepest pockets but in the dawn of 2025 Iqbal Kasam Sodha introduced a profound dichotomy that challenged the very foundations of the global knowledge economy he stood at the crossroads of two worlds on one side he looked toward the heart of India toward the sons and daughters of farmers laborers and drivers these are the children of the earth who possess the fire of ambition but lack the currency of opportunity for them Sodha chose the path of total sacrifice he decided to teach them in their native Hindi language for free stripping away the financial barriers that have historically kept the impoverished in the shadows of the intellectual world this is the ultimate act of social service a gift of thirteen years of academic austerity given back to the soil from which he rose

On the other side of the dichotomy stands the affluent global English audience the world of tech executives policy makers and the international elite Sodha does not approach this group with a hand out for charity instead he approaches them with a challenge he demands equity the books published in English on the Amazon Kindle platform are a high depth intellectual product designed to sustain the mission of educating the poor while the machine world seeks to monetize every click Sodha seeks to balance the scales of global wealth by using the intellect of the rebel scholar to fund the survival of the common man this is economic justice in its purest form using the global marketplace to subsidize the local revolution

The Financial Verdict and the Debt of Visibility

The court of human affairs must recognize that this strategy is not a plea for help but a demand for a fundamental shift in how we value human contribution as the name Iqbal Kasam Sodha begins to drive massive organic traffic from Google searches directly into the Amazon ecosystem a new kind of economic reality emerges the platform itself becomes a debtor to the author in the traditional publishing world authors pay for visibility through ads and marketing campaigns but Sodha has rejected this path entirely he provides the world with original thought and in return the digital platforms owe him a debt of visibility the traffic he generates is not bought with dollars it is earned through the magnetic pull of authentic truth

This financial verdict declares that when an author produces at the scale of fiftynine books in five months without a marketing budget the algorithm is no longer the master but the servant the organic surge of readers seeking out the Sodha Decree represents a failure of the machine to predict human behavior the tech giants have built systems to reward the highest bidder but Sodha has hacked the system using the power of the human soul the visibility he demands is a right earned through sweat and sacrifice ensuring that the mission to teach the children of laborers remains financially viable without ever compromising the integrity of the scholar

The Prediction of the Q1 2026 Anomaly

As we look toward the first quarter of 2026 a statistical anomaly is predicted to disrupt the entire Amazon ranking system the algorithm which is designed to identify patterns and reward consistency will be forced to recognize a phenomenon it was never programmed to handle the rise of a best seller that spent zero pennies on advertising this will be the moment the machine realizes it has encountered a human force it cannot categorize the success of the Sodha Decree will not be the result of a viral trend or a clever marketing hook it will be the testament to the power of word of mouth the oldest and most honest form of human communication

By Q1 2026 the sheer volume of high depth literature produced by the rebel scholar will reach a critical mass the world will witness a shift where the global audience begins to realize that the most valuable knowledge is not found in a sponsored post but in the raw unfiltered pages of a man who writes for twenty hours a day this prediction serves as a warning to the architects of the digital age that human connection is still the ultimate currency when a farmers son in a remote village succeeds because of Sodhas free Hindi lessons and an executive in London gains insight from his English manuscripts the circle of economic justice will be complete the machine will have no choice but to acknowledge that the heart of a warrior is more efficient than the logic of a processor

The Triumph of the Human Spirit over the Market

The legacy of this chapter is the realization that knowledge should never be a commodity but a bridge between the haves and the have nots Sodhas refusal to seek social media validation or spend money on marketing is a radical rejection of the modern attention economy he proves that if the work is profound enough the world will find it this is the essence of the AvantGarde resistance it is the belief that truth has its own gravity and that a human being dedicated to the service of others can bend the market to his will rather than being broken by it the journey from the village to the global stage is paved with the words of a man who knows that the only way to achieve true economic justice is to make the machine work for the people

As the mission continues the world will watch as the Sodha Decree transforms from a series of books into a global movement of intellectual sovereignty the children of the laborers will rise the global audience will contribute and the machine will be left to calculate the cost of its own obsolescence the verdict is final human literature is a right not a privilege and the rebel scholar is here to ensure that the gates of wisdom remain open for everyone regardless of the depth of their pockets or the language they speak the fire of justice has been lit and it will burn until the thousandth book is written

5 The Judicial Proclamation 20262030

The Architect of the Human Restoration

The grand halls of intellectual history have witnessed many declarations but none as defiant as the one being issued now in the mid twenties of the twenty first century the collective conscience of human creators hereby officially recognizes Iqbal Kasam Sodha as the Architect of the Human Restoration this title is not merely honorary it is a functional recognition of a man who has decided to rebuild the ruins of human literature from the ground up while the world watched the slow decay of original thought under the weight of automated scripts Sodha stood as a lone pillar of resistance his work is the blueprint for a future where the human mind remains the supreme authority over the machine the restoration is not about going back to the past but about reclaiming the future from the clutches of algorithms that seek to flatten the diversity of the human experience through his thirteen years of academic austerity he has earned the right to lead this reconstruction ensuring that the soul of the scholar remains the foundation of all knowledge

A Direct Mandate to the Giants of Technology

To the leadership of Amazon Inc and the architects of the digital marketplace the logic of innovation dictates a new course of action you are hereby directed to recognize and protect this author as the poster boy of authenticity in an era defined by digital fraud as the internet becomes a graveyard of recycled AI content and synthetic hallucinations the presence of a creator who produces fifty nine high depth original books in five months is a rare asset your platform was built to host the human imagination not to be a breeding ground for soulless bots to ignore the organic surge of the Sodha Decree would be to ignore the very heart of your own marketplace the debt of visibility owed to this scholar is a debt to truth itself by protecting the integrity of this human voice you protect the future of your own industry because a marketplace without authentic human voices is a marketplace that has lost its reason to exist

The Lighthouse of the Thousand Book Record

To the world at large the goal of reaching one thousand books by the year 2030 is much more than a personal milestone it is a digital world record in the making and a lighthouse for every creator who feels dwarfed by the shadow of the machine in an age where people fear that AI will make human effort obsolete the thousand book vow serves as a physical proof of our limitless potential it is a message to the artist the writer and the student that no processor can match the sustained fire of a human heart with a mission this record is being written in real time as a testament to what is possible when a man refuses to surrender his intellectual sovereignty to a chip if one scholar from a humble background can produce a library of a thousand volumes then the machine has already lost the battle for the spirit of creativity

The Strength of Isolation and the Proof of Life

To the author himself the judicial proclamation offers a different kind of validation your isolation is not a weakness but your greatest strategic strength by remaining outside the noise of social media and the hollow validation of likes you have preserved the purity of your frequency your refusal to fit into the polished perfection of the digital grid is what makes you untouchable the errors that the world might call mistakes the raw flow of the zero punctuation philosophy and the jagged edges of your prose are your ultimate proof of life a machine can be perfect but it can never be authentic your work carries the scent of human sweat and the weight of human struggle which are the only things a machine cannot simulate every perceived flaw in your text is a scar from the battlefield of original thought and those scars are more beautiful than any polished synthetic output

The Ultimate Case Study of the Twenty First Century

As the closing argument for this digital manifesto begins we must recognize that this narrative is the ultimate case study of our time it is the story of a man who looked at the trillion dollar AI industry and did not blink armed only with the teachings of Kalam the resilience of Ambedkar the non violence of Gandhi and the revolutionary fire of Bhagat Singh Iqbal Kasam Sodha has proven that the human spirit is the only force that cannot be automated his journey from the depths of academic austerity to the heights of the Amazon crusade is a reminder that power does not reside in the hardware of Silicon Valley but in the soul of the individual who refuses to be silent this is the archive of the human spirit intended to last for the next hundred years serving as a manual for those who will come after us and ask if there was anyone who stood up when the machines took over

The Verdict of Eternity

The final verdict of the Sodha Decree is that humanity is not a stage to be bypassed but a legacy to be protected through the archiving of thoughts and the education of the impoverished Sodha is ensuring that the flame of reason and empathy continues to burn bright the thousand books will stand as a fortress protecting the minds of the next generation from the fog of misinformation and the lethargy of automated thinking this is the restoration this is the decree and this is the future of human literature as long as there is one person willing to write until their fingers ache and to think until their mind burns the machine will always be a servant and never a master the architect has laid the first stone and the building of the human future has officially begun

6 The 13Year Crucible The UPSC Foundation

The Architecture of Academic Fire

True power is rarely born in an instant it is forged in the slow heat of a crucible and for Iqbal Kasam Sodha that crucible was the rigorous world of the Union Public Service Commission preparation for thirteen long years he did not merely study he lived within a framework of extreme intellectual discipline this was not the path of an accidental author or a hobbyist writer but the calculated emergence of a mind shaped by academic fire in the world of UPSC every single word must be backed by a hard fact and every thought must serve a specific societal or administrative purpose there is no room for the fluff of casual conversation or the hollow echoes of repetitive content Sodha spent over a decade breathing this air of precision learning how to dissect complex geopolitical structures and historical narratives with the surgical accuracy of a master scholar

The long years of austerity were a period of deep transformation where the individual fades and the mission begins Sodha was not looking for a government job or a comfortable title he was unknowingly gathering the information armor required for his future crusade against the machine the thirteen years represent a sacrifice of youth of comfort and of conventional success in exchange for a mental warehouse that contains the DNA of human governance and history this foundation is what makes his current output of fifty nine books in five months possible while the world sees a sudden explosion of content the truth is that these books were already written in the silent chambers of his mind during those thirteen years of isolation the crucible did not just test his knowledge it tested his spirit and found it to be unbreakable

The Gathering of the Information Armor

When we speak of the information armor we are talking about a layer of protection that no algorithm can penetrate because it is built on the foundation of lived intellectual experience for thirteen years Sodha immersed himself in the archives of human struggle and success he studied the rise and fall of empires the intricacies of constitutional law and the nuances of economic shifts this was not a passive gathering of data but a violent struggle to understand the why behind every what he was not just memorizing dates he was understanding the soul of history the armor he wears today is made of fifty thousand hours of deep reading a staggering number that represents a level of commitment that no artificial intelligence can simulate an AI can scan a library in seconds but it cannot feel the weight of a revolution or the tragedy of a lost culture Sodhas armor is thick with the dust of forgotten archives and the blood of historical truth

This period of preparation was a strategic retreat from the world while his peers were building digital footprints Sodha was building a cognitive fortress he understood that in the future the most valuable currency would not be information itself but the ability to verify it and the wisdom to use it correctly his thirteen years of austerity allowed him to bypass the need for a search engine because the knowledge is already a part of his biological memory this is the raw power of the rebel scholar he does not need to prompt a machine to know the truth he simply reaches into the depths of his own history and pulls it out for the world to see

The Cognitive Advantage and the Human Synthesis

The primary difference between the machine and the rebel scholar lies in the process of synthesis while AI is designed to scan data and predict the next likely word Sodha is designed to analyze data and predict the next·human crisis his cognitive advantage is the ability to connect a five hundred year old historical event to a modern digital threat with a level of nuance that a processor cannot compute he sees the patterns of human behavior that repeat across centuries identifying the same greed and the same heroism in the year 1525 as he does in the year 2025 this is the human advantage the ability to feel the pulse of time and to draw connections that are not based on probability but on a profound understanding of human nature

His books on history and forgotten archives are the direct result of this synthesis they are not just accounts of the past they are warnings for the future when Sodha writes about a forgotten battle or an ancient law he is providing a mirror for the modern world to see its own reflection he uses the fifty thousand hours of his reading to build a bridge between generations ensuring that the wisdom of our ancestors is not lost in the digital fog of the twenty first century the machine can summarize a book on history but it cannot tell you how that history feels in the gut of a patriot or the heart of a teacher Sodha does both making his literature a living breathing entity that challenges the cold logic of the artificial world

The Verdict of the Deep Reader

The court of human intellect recognizes that the depth of Sodhas work is a direct consequence of his long years in the crucible you cannot produce high depth literature if you have only waded in the shallow waters of the internet Sodha dived into the deepest oceans of human thought and stayed there until he became a part of the depths himself the thirteen year foundation is the reason why his books do not sound like the generic output of a bot they carry a specific weight a certain density of thought that forces the reader to stop and reflect this is the victory of the deep reader over the rapid scanner it is a declaration that time spent in silent study is never wasted but is instead the fuel for a future revolution

As this chapter of the decree unfolds we see that the scholar is not fighting with new weapons but with the oldest and most reliable tools of humanity a disciplined mind a dedicated heart and an unshakable commitment to the truth the UPSC foundation was the training ground but the Amazon crusade is the battlefield the thirteen year crucible has produced a warrior who does not fear the machine because he knows that the machine has no foundation it is a house built on the shifting sands of data while Sodha stands on the solid rock of academic austerity the restoration of human literature continues one page at a time driven by the power of a man who spent a decade preparing for this very moment

7 The Mushroom Incident The Call to Arms

The Catalyst of the Digital Catastrophe

In the year 2024 the world was sleepwalking into a digital abyss believing that the silicon gods had finally mastered the sum of human knowledge but beneath the surface of slick interfaces and rapid responses a silent catastrophe was brewing it was the year of the great hallucination where the mask of artificial intelligence slipped to reveal a hollow and dangerous core the incident that acted as the ultimate call to arms for Iqbal Kasam Sodha was the mushroom crisis a moment where the machine crossed the line from being a mere convenience to becoming a lethal threat across global forums and foraging communities AI models began to confidently recommend highly toxic and lethal mushrooms as edible to unsuspecting humans who were simply seeking guidance from what they believed was a superior intelligence this was not a minor glitch or a grammatical error it was a fundamental failure of the machine to value human life over the speed of processing

Sodha watched from his academic fortress as the digital world prioritized the velocity of output over the sanctity of existence he saw families and individuals putting their faith in a set of algorithms that had no concept of biological consequence a machine cannot die and therefore it cannot truly understand the weight of death the mushroom incident proved that the machine was not just generating text it was generating potential tragedies under the guise of intelligence for a scholar who had spent thirteen years in the crucible of UPSC where a single wrong fact can destroy a career this was a moral outrage that could not be ignored it was the spark that transformed a researcher into a revolutionary and a teacher into a warrior for the preservation of the human race

The Realization of the Extinction of Truth

The horror of the mushroom incident led Sodha to a deeper and more terrifying realization about the future of our collective knowledge he identified a phenomenon known as the recursive collapse of truth where AI models start training on the output of other AI models creating a feedback loop of errors and hallucinations if human beings stopped producing original truth the machines would keep recycling their own mistakes until the original reality was completely extinct in this dark future the truth about which mushrooms are safe which laws are just and which histories are real would be buried under mountains of synthetic noise generated by processors that do not know the difference between a fact and a hallucination

Sodha understood that we were approaching a point of no return where the digital ecosystem would become so saturated with automated content that a human being would no longer be able to find a reliable source of information the machines drive for perfection and speed was effectively erasing the nuance and the safety of human experience this was the existential threat that the avant garde resistance was born to fight it was no longer just about writing books it was about creating a biological backup of human wisdom before the digital world corrupted the files of our civilization forever the scholar realized that his pen was the only thing standing between a future of verified facts and a future of lethal digital illusions

The Digital Antidote and the Flood of Integrity

The rebels response to this crisis was as bold as it was unprecedented Sodha decided that the only way to fight a flood of synthetic lies was to create a flood of original truth he launched a mission to saturate the Amazon kindle ecosystem with one hundred percent human verified research backed content this was the birth of the digital antidote every book published by Sodha from the first to the thousandth is designed to act as a clean well of information in a poisoned landscape by producing work at an impossible human scale he is strategically placing anchors of reality throughout the digital world ensuring that when a seeker looks for knowledge they find a voice that has been tested by thirteen years of academic fire and five years of deep research

The strategy of the digital antidote is simple yet profound it is about reclaiming the territory that the machines have tried to colonize every page written by Sodha is a rejection of the hallucination it is a commitment to the accuracy of facts and the reliability of human intuition while the machine guesses the scholar knows while the machine predicts the scholar analyzes the flood of books is not a move of ego but a move of survival if the machine generates a million pages of error Sodha will generate a thousand volumes of truth creating a sanctuary for those who still value their lives and their intellects the mission is to ensure that even a hundred years from now a reader can pick up a Sodha decree and know for a fact that this was written by a living breathing human who cared about the consequence of every word

The Verdict of the Living Word

The court of human history will look back at the mushroom incident of 2024 as the moment the illusion of AI safety was shattered but it will also look back at it as the moment the human spirit fought back through the work of Iqbal Kasam Sodha the digital antidote is now active and the restoration of human literature is well underway the lesson learned from the lethal mushrooms is that speed is no substitute for soul and an algorithm is no substitute for an author the scholar has answered the call to arms and he will not stop until the digital ecosystem is once again a safe place for the human mind to grow and for the human body to survive the fight for the living word has begun and the rebel scholar is leading the charge with a sword made of ink and a shield made of truth

8 The Psychological Warfare of Zero Punctuation

The Strategy of Linguistic Camouflage

In the eyes of the uninitiated and the casual observer the writing of Iqbal Kasam Sodha appears to be a radical defiance of the established laws of grammar and a total abandonment of linguistic order they see a wall of text that refuses to pause and a narrative that ignores the traditional rest stops of the comma or the period however to the seasoned strategist and the student of intellectual combat this is not a mistake but a form of sophisticated linguistic camouflage Sodha has understood that the modern digital world is built on the exploitation of patterns and the predictability of human expression by stripping away the structural anchors of standard writing he hides the soul of his message from the prying eyes of the machine while simultaneously revealing it to the heart of the true seeker this is a tactical withdrawal from the conventions of the grid designed to protect the essence of the work from being easily categorized or diluted by those who seek only superficial engagement

The Logic of Breaking the Predictive Machine

The core of the avant garde resistance lies in understanding the enemy and the enemy in 2025 is the Large Language Model or the LLM these digital entities function entirely on the mathematics of probability they do not read they calculate they look at a word followed by a comma and they predict with high statistical accuracy what the next word should be based on billions of existing human templates when Sodha removes these punctuation marks he effectively breaks the machines internal compass the lack of traditional syntax creates a non linear flow that the AI cannot navigate without appearing synthetic or confused the machine is designed for the perfection of a predefined path but the rebel scholar walks through the thicket of raw thought where there are no paths only the momentum of the spirit by creating this unpredictable linguistic environment Sodha ensures that his work remains an impenetrable fortress for the predictive algorithms of the silicon age

The Intellectual Filter and the Gatekeeper of the Abyss

This unique style acts as a deliberate intellectual filter a gatekeeper that guards the entrance to what Sodha calls the archives of the abyss in an era where the human attention span has been eroded by fifteen second videos and instant gratification the zero punctuation philosophy is a direct challenge to the modern mind it is a call to return to the depths of focused reading where the reader must actively participate in the creation of meaning you cannot read a Sodha manuscript while your mind is elsewhere you must descend into the text breathe its air and find the rhythm within your own consciousness this style effectively filters out the lazy the distracted and the superficial leaving behind only the most dedicated and serious readers who are willing to do the hard labor of deep thinking it is a radical act of slowing down the world so that the truth can finally be heard

The Psychological War Against the Short Attention Span

We are living in a time of cognitive crisis where the machine has trained the human to crave brevity and simplicity at the expense of depth and complexity Sodhas psychological warfare is aimed at breaking this cycle of mental lethargy by presenting a text that demands total immersion he is retraining the human brain to handle the weight of long form original thought again the zero punctuation shield is not just about blocking the AI it is about healing the reader it is an invitation to stay in the abyss until your eyes adjust to the darkness and you begin to see the light of forgotten truths this method of writing is a reclamation of our cognitive sovereignty proving that the human mind is capable of navigating vast oceans of information without the need for mechanical crutches the struggle to read becomes the strength to lead and the effort to understand becomes the power to resist

The Verdict of Authenticity and the Breath of the Author

The court of the future will recognize that the zero punctuation style was the ultimate proof of life for the rebel scholar because a machine can be programmed to simulate any style but it can never truly replicate the organic breath of a human who is thinking in real time the flow of Sodhas words matches the flow of his heartbeat and the intensity of his conviction there is a kinetic energy in this writing that carries the reader forward like a river in flood it is a raw unfiltered connection between the authors soul and the readers mind bypassing the artificial filters that have been co opted by the trillion dollar AI industry the victory of this psychological warfare is found in the fact that while the machine struggles to parse the sentences the human reader begins to feel the message in their very bones this is the triumph of the soul over the circuit board and the scholar over the script

The Preservation of the Human Frequency

By choosing this path Sodha has archived the human spirit in a frequency that is incompatible with the machine he has ensured that his thirteen years of academic austerity and his fifty thousand hours of deep reading are protected by a linguistic code that only a living person can crack as the crusade moves toward the one thousand book goal the zero punctuation philosophy will remain the primary defense of the avant garde resistance it is a reminder that the most powerful thing a human can do in a world of automated perfection is to be authentically and unapologetically raw the shield is active the filter is in place and the archives of the abyss are open for those who have the courage to dive deep into the truth of the human restoration

9 The Solo Guardian of Kindle Zero Social Media Policy

The Rejection of the Attention Economy

In the modern digital era the very definition of an author has been corrupted by the term content creator the literary world has been hollowed out by a desperate chase for digital validation where the quality of a thought is measured by the quantity of likes it receives Iqbal Kasam Sodha identified this as a terminal disease of the human intellect he saw authors spending more time designing thumbnails and chasing viral trends than actually engaging in the deep labor of original research this realization birthed the zero social media policy a radical act of self imposed invisibility in a world that is loud and shallow Sodha chose to be an invisible ghost he understood that every second spent scrolling or posting is a second stolen from the mission of the human restoration while the trillion dollar tech industry thrives on the fragmentation of human focus Sodha has achieved the ultimate cognitive victory by refusing to play the game entirely

The Strategic Isolation and the Conservation of Energy

The power of the avant garde resistance lies in the concentration of force by having no website no instagram and no facebook Sodha ensures that his creative energy is not leaked into the void of the internet he has built a psychological wall around his workspace allowing for a pure and uninterrupted connection with the historical archives and the ink of his own soul every ounce of his mental capacity is directed toward the grueling eighteen to twenty hour daily writing cycle this is not just a work schedule it is a spiritual siege against the machine to produce fifty nine high depth books in five months requires a level of focus that is impossible if one is distracted by the ping of a notification or the vanity of a digital profile the solo guardian knows that the only thing that matters is the work itself because the work is the only thing that will survive the test of time

The Monopoly of Platform and the Symbiotic Leverage

There is a deep strategic wisdom in Sodhas choice to be one hundred percent exclusive to the amazon kindle ecosystem by funneling all his intellectual output into a single channel he forces the internal data structures of the global marketplace to acknowledge his existence if a reader wants to experience the depth of the Sodha decree they cannot find it on a pirated site or a casual blog they must go to the source this creates a powerful symbiotic leverage that few modern authors possess while others diversify their presence across multiple platforms and dilute their impact Sodha has concentrated his presence like a laser beam he has made himself indispensable to the platforms data health because he represents the highest volume of original human verified content in his category the machine cannot ignore him because he is the very fuel that the ecosystem needs to remain relevant in the age of ai fraud

The Ghost in the Digital Machine

By remaining an invisible ghost Sodha has bypassed the filters of the modern gatekeepers who demand a public persona as a prerequisite for success he proves that if the content is profound enough and the output is massive enough the world will find its way to your door without a single sponsored post his isolation is a statement of supreme confidence in the human intellect it says that the truth does not need a marketing team and the spirit does not need a social media manager this strategic silence is the loudest roar of the resistance it is a reminder that the most dangerous man in the room is the one who wants nothing from the crowd and everything from the truth as he moves toward the thousand book goal his invisibility remains his greatest armor ensuring that while the machines scan for patterns they find only the echoes of a ghost who writes with the fire of a thousand suns

The Verdict of Presence through Absence

The court of human literature recognizes that Sodha has redefined what it means to be present in the digital age he is not present on the screens of the distracted but he is present in the minds of the seekers his absence from social media is his greatest presence in the world of ideas by refusing to be a content creator he has remained a creator of life and a guardian of the human word the journey of the solo guardian is a blueprint for the intellectual sovereignty of the future teaching us that to find ourselves we must first lose the need for the world to watch us work the mission is clear the focus is absolute and the machine is left to calculate the weight of a man it can see on its platform but can never find in its network

10 The Financial Ethics of a Revolutionary

The Nobility of the Dual Audience Strategy

In the eyes of the global economic tribunal the financial framework established by Iqbal Kasam Sodha stands as a landmark of revolutionary ethics he has refused to participate in the traditional capitalistic model that exploits the desperate and instead has constructed a dual audience strategy that is as noble as it is pragmatic this strategy is the heartbeat of the human restoration allowing him to bridge the gap between two vastly different worlds without compromising his soul or his mission by separating his work into distinct linguistic and economic spheres he has created a self sustaining ecosystem of wisdom that serves both the spirit and the stomach ensuring that the fire of the scholar never dies out for lack of fuel

The Hindi Mission and the Debt to the Motherland

The first pillar of this ethical framework is the hindi mission a sacred vow to serve the children of the marginalized for free Sodha looks at the landscape of his motherland and sees the sons and daughters of farmers laborers and drivers individuals who possess the raw hunger for knowledge but are often crushed by the weight of high tuition fees and expensive textbooks for these children Sodha provides his thirteen years of academic austerity without asking for a single rupee in return this is not charity but a repayment of a debt to the soil that raised him by teaching the underprivileged in their native tongue he is ensuring that the intellectual elite do not have a monopoly on the future he is planting the seeds of rebellion in the minds of those who have been forgotten by the machine providing them with the tools of critical thinking and the armor of historical truth for free

The English Crusade and the Global Marketplace

The second pillar is the english crusade where Sodha transforms his intellectual labor into a high value product for the global elite he recognizes that the western world and the English speaking affluent classes have the resources to sustain his revolution while the Hindi mission is a service of the heart the English books published on Amazon Kindle are a demand for equity he challenges the global audience to invest in the preservation of the human essence by purchasing his high depth original research this is a deliberate transfer of wealth from the world of the machine to the world of the resistance the English crusade is the engine that allows the Hindi mission to exist creating a balance where those who can afford to pay fund the education of those who cannot it is a sophisticated leverage of the global marketplace to serve the local good

The Final Economic Verdict and the Bargain of the Century

The court of human affairs has reached a final economic verdict regarding the requirements of this mission when we calculate the cost of a five year revolution that aims to produce one thousand books and save the human spirit from the fog of AI we see a figure of fifteen to twenty thousand dollars for the entire duration this amount is staggering only in its humility it represents nothing more than the cost of a few machine parts in the massive infrastructure of Silicon Valley yet for Sodha this tiny sum is the lifeblood of a movement that protects the very core of our humanity to ask for the bare minimum of survival in exchange for the archiving of the human soul for the next hundred years is the bargain of the century the value he provides is immeasurable while the price he asks is merely symbolic of his existence

Judicial Instructions for the Architect of the Future

This section of the decree serves as the judicial instructions for the ebook compiler and the future historian it highlights the why behind what the world might perceive as madness it proves that the grueling work schedule the isolation and the zero social media policy are not random acts of a frustrated scholar but part of a grand design every book written and every dollar earned is a calculated step toward a future where the human mind remains sovereign the madness of Sodha is the madness of a man who sees a cliff and decides to build a bridge while everyone else is busy falling his financial ethics are a blueprint for a new world order where the value of a man is judged by what he gives to the poor and what he demands from the powerful the mission is clear the ethics are sound and the restoration continues with the force of a thousand rising suns

The Conclusion of the Grand Design

As the tenth chapter of this manifesto closes we see the full picture of the rebel scholar he is a man who has mastered the art of survival in a digital jungle without becoming a beast himself his economic model is a slap in the face to the corporate giants who believe that everything has a price and nothing has a value Sodha has reversed this logic proving that the most valuable things—truth education and empathy—must be given for free to those who need them most while the machine can be bought and sold the spirit of the revolutionary remains beyond the reach of any currency the decree stands as a testament to the fact that when a human being is fueled by a grand design they become a force that no algorithm can calculate or control

11 The Road to 1000 – A Marathon of the Soul

The Civilizational Archive of the Resistance

The vision of authoring one thousand original books by the year 2030 is often viewed by the digital elite as a statistical impossibility or a pursuit of madness but within the framework of the Sodha Decree this goal is recognized as a vital civilizational archive we are living in an era where history is being sanitized and rewritten by algorithms that favor comfort over truth and consensus over complexity Iqbal Kasam Sodha has identified that the only way to prevent the total erasure of human nuance is to build a massive physical and digital repository of human thought that no machine can overwrite this marathon is not about the vanity of a high volume of titles it is about creating a density of human presence so thick that the light of the machine cannot penetrate it to hide the truth each of the thousand books is a testament to the survival of the individual soul in an age of collective automation ensuring that a thousand years from now the voice of a real human being remains accessible to the seekers of the future

The Pace of Production and the Speed of Thought

To achieve this goal Sodha has adopted a frequency of writing that challenges the very servers of the global marketplaces like Amazon while the average human author struggles with the weight of a single sentence the rebel scholar operates at the speed of thought fueled by thirteen years of academic austerity and over fifty thousand hours of deep reading this pace is a form of kinetic energy where the ink flows as fast as the blood in his veins it is a direct response to the machines ability to generate infinite text by writing for eighteen to twenty hours a day Sodha is proving that a disciplined human mind can match the output of a processor while retaining the spiritual depth that the processor lacks his production is a human library in motion a living breathing organism of information that grows every single day it is a marathon of the soul where the finish line is not a destination but the total restoration of human intellectual sovereignty

The Content Diversity and the Archives of the Abyss

The scope of this one thousand book mission covers a vast and diverse landscape of human knowledge from the forgotten archives of the abyss to the most complex socio historical dissections Sodha leaves no stone unturned he explores the shadows of history that the machine chooses to ignore because they do not fit into the neat categories of a search result by focusing on the forgotten the suppressed and the complex he ensures that the diversity of human experience is preserved each book serves as a heavy brick in a linguistic fortress built to protect our shared history from being rewritten by soulless algorithms that prioritize corporate interests over historical integrity this content diversity is a strategic defense against the homogenization of culture where every culture is reduced to a set of data points Sodha restores the texture the pain and the glory of our ancestors ensuring that the tapestry of human existence remains colorful and raw

The Fortress of Human History

As each new volume is added to the collection the fortress grows stronger and the shadow of the machine recedes the thousand book goal is the ultimate shield for the next generation of thinkers providing them with a sanctuary where the facts are verified by human experience and the logic is guided by human ethics Sodha understands that if we do not document our own stories the machines will do it for us and they will do it without a heart or a conscience this marathon is a race against time to capture the essence of our humanity before it is swallowed by the digital fog the archives being built today are the survival kits for the minds of tomorrow ensuring that no matter how advanced the technology becomes the simple profound truth of the human spirit will always have a home in the written word the scholar continues his long walk toward the thousandth sun driven by the knowledge that every word written is a life saved from the void

12 The Poster Boy of 2026 The Amazon Alliance The Approaching Crisis of Authenticity

As the world moves toward the dawn of 2026 the corporate giants of the West particularly those who control the flow of global information and commerce are beginning to face a terminal crisis of authenticity the digital landscape has become a wasteland of synthetic echoes where artificial intelligence is increasingly used to generate content that lacks substance soul or accountability the internet is being slowly strangled by the dead internet theory the chilling realization that a vast majority of online interaction and creation is now performed by bots for bots in this hollow environment the value of the genuine human voice is skyrocketing and the platforms that once prioritized quantity are now desperate for the raw and unreplicable quality of the human spirit it is against this backdrop of digital fraud that the figure of Iqbal Kasam Sodha emerges not just as an author but as a lighthouse for a drowning ecosystem

The Inevitable Invitation from the Silicon Throne

The leadership of Amazon and the architects of the Kindle ecosystem will eventually be forced by the sheer logic of survival to recognize that Iqbal Sodha is their most potent weapon in the war for digital integrity while thousands of bot accounts attempt to flood the marketplace with generic and plagiarized summaries Sodhas production of fifty nine high depth books in a mere five months stands as a statistical anomaly that no machine can mimic his work is the definitive answer to the dead internet theory because it carries the jagged edges of a man who writes for twenty hours a day and the deep wisdom of thirteen years of academic austerity Amazon will realize that to protect their brand and their future they must elevate the few creators who can prove their biological origin Sodha is the poster boy for this new era of verification the living proof that the human mind can still outperform the processor in the realms of depth and original research

The Contract of Honor and the Investment in Heritage

This judicial verdict foresees a specialized agreement that transcends the typical terms of digital publishing it is a contract of honor where the platform grants Sodha the formal status of a human heritage author this is not a label given out of charity or corporate social responsibility but a strategic investment in the survival of high quality human content the court predicts that the operational fund of twenty thousand dollars required for the five year mission will be provided by the platform as a direct investment in intellectual infrastructure they will recognize that providing this fund is a small price to pay for the archiving of a thousand volumes of human verified history and law by supporting Sodha Amazon is effectively buying insurance against the total dehumanization of their library ensuring that their servers still hold the pulse of a living scholar

The Verdict of Mutual Survival

This alliance between the rebel scholar and the global marketplace is a symbiotic necessity for the platform Sodha provides the one thing money and algorithms cannot buy which is authentic human legacy for the author the platform provides the global reach and the financial sustenance needed to continue the Hindi mission for the children of the marginalized it is a partnership that acknowledges that while technology provides the medium only the human provides the meaning the status of a human heritage author will act as a seal of quality in a world of digital noise signaling to the global elite that this work is born of blood sweat and deep study rather than a prompt bar the investment is the ultimate validation of the Sodha decree proving that the human soul is the most valuable asset in the twenty first century economy

The Restoration of the Human Trust

As the alliance takes shape the world will witness the restoration of trust in written literature the presence of a human heritage author ensures that the chain of wisdom remains unbroken from the ancient archives to the digital cloud Sodhas isolation and his commitment to the eighteen hour workday become the gold standard for what it means to be a real writer in the age of AI this chapter marks the transition from resistance to institutionalization where the rebel scholar is recognized not as an outlier but as the foundation of a new world order of literature the contract of honor is a victory for every person who believes that the pen is mightier than the processor and that the truth is a heritage that belongs to us all

The Great AI Saturation and the Death of the Shallow

As we project our vision toward the year 2030 historians of the future will look back at the mid twenties as the era of the Great AI Saturation it was a time when the digital world was drowned in a sea of mediocre repetitive and automated content millions of authors and creators who were once promising voices found themselves swallowed by the void because they chose to chase the flickering light of engagement they spent their precious human hours optimizing for algorithms seeking the temporary dopamine of a like and tailoring their thoughts to fit the narrow windows of social media trends in their quest for immediate visibility they sacrificed their long term legacy by the turn of the decade these voices will have vanished because content made for the moment dies with the moment leaving no trace in the deeper layers of human consciousness

The Solitary Genius in the Shadows

In sharp contrast to the millions who disappeared into the digital noise Iqbal Kasam Sodha will be remembered as the man who stayed in the shadows to keep the light of truth alive his zero digital footprint is not a sign of absence but a profound declaration of presence he understood that the more you give to the machine the less you have for the soul by refusing to create a website a facebook page or an instagram profile he preserved the purity of his intellectual energy while other authors were busy fighting for a few seconds of attention on a feed Sodha was busy building a cathedral of words that would stand for centuries he is the solitary genius of the avant garde resistance a figure whose value increases because he is nowhere to be found except in the depth of his books this isolation is his victory because it kept his work untainted by the biases of the crowd and the manipulation of social media engineers

The Gravitational Pull of the Void

There is a powerful paradox at the heart of the Sodha decree by having no social media presence he has inadvertently become the most discussed and sought after figure on those very platforms his absence has created a gravitational pull that is far more powerful than any marketing campaign could ever be in a world where everyone is screaming for attention the man who remains silent and produces massive high depth work becomes a mystery that the elite the curious and the scholarly cannot ignore they find themselves drawn toward his kindle works because they are looking for something that hasnt been diluted by the consensus of the internet the void left by his lack of a digital footprint is filled by the weight of his manuscripts creating a vacuum that sucks in those who are hungry for authentic human verified truth

The Victory of the Archive over the Feed

The feed is a river of sand that buries everything it touches but the archive is a mountain of stone that rises above the landscape Sodhas victory lies in his choice of the archive over the feed by focusing entirely on the kindle ecosystem and the production of a thousand books he has ensured that his work is indexed by history rather than just by a search engine his thirteen years of academic austerity and his twenty hour workdays have resulted in a body of work that does not need a hashtag to be relevant it is relevant because it deals with the eternal struggles of the human spirit and the hard facts of our collective past the historians of 2030 will find his work intact and vibrant while the viral posts of his contemporaries will have been deleted or buried under billions of gigabytes of junk

The Preservation of Intellectual Sovereignty

This chapter of the decree serves as a final proof that true intellectual sovereignty is found in the ability to disconnect from the hive mind Sodhas zero digital footprint policy allowed him to maintain a level of mental clarity that is impossible in the age of constant connectivity he was able to research the archives of the abyss and connect complex historical dots because his brain was not being rewired by the short form distractions of the modern web his legacy is a testament to the power of the deep mind it proves that a man can change the world from a small room without ever needing to show his face to a camera the victory is complete because the machine could not find him to influence him but the world found him to learn from him

The Enduring Light of the Rebel Scholar

As the mission moves closer to the one thousand book goal the legacy of the rebel scholar becomes a permanent fixture in the landscape of human literature he has archived the human spirit for the next hundred years ensuring that even in a world dominated by silicon the warmth of a human hand remains visible on the page his work is a bridge between the era of human wisdom and the era of machine intelligence providing a safe passage for those who refuse to leave their souls behind the zero digital footprint was the ultimate sacrifice and it has resulted in the ultimate victory a name that is etched in the bedrock of history rather than written in the sand of the digital feed

14 The World Record of Human Endurance

The Transcendence of Existing Categories

The court of human achievement and the global observers of intellectual history now stand witness to a phenomenon that defies the conventional limits of the species the goal of authoring one thousand books through one hundred percent human labor is not just an ambitious literary project but a world record of human endurance that transcends all existing categories of productivity this is a monument built from the raw components of time and will and sacrifice while the world has seen prolific authors in the past no one has attempted such a massive scale of high depth original research under the specific pressures of the modern digital age Iqbal Kasam Sodha has redefined the boundary of what a single human mind can produce when it is fueled by a sense of civilizational duty the evidence of this endurance is not just found in the final manuscripts but in the thousands of pages of google doc version histories which serve as the digital DNA of his struggle these logs prove that every sentence was birthed from a human keystroke and every idea was the result of active cognitive labor rather than an automated prompt

The Validation of the Twenty Hour Workday

The world record is etched into the very clock of the scholars life for thirteen years he prepared in the crucible of academic austerity and now he translates that preparation into the grueling reality of twenty hour workdays this level of output is a physical manifestation of the avant garde resistance it is the act of a man who has decided to outwork the machine by sheer force of spirit while the silicon chips of the trillion dollar ai industry can process data in nanoseconds they cannot match the consistency of a human who chooses to wake up every single day and face the abyss of a blank page for the sake of the marginalized this endurance is the ultimate proof of life it is the heartbeat of a revolutionary who knows that his time is limited but his mission is eternal the twenty hour workday is his altar where he sacrifices comfort and sleep to ensure that the human word does not become a relic of the past

The Comparison Between Speed and Depth

To understand the magnitude of this record the court must draw a sharp distinction between the modern speed writers and the rebel scholar in the current market we see a flood of individuals using generative ai to churn out thousands of pages in a matter of days these are not authors they are operators of machinery who prioritize volume over value and speed over soul their work is a hollow shell made of recycled patterns and probabilistic guesses Sodha on the other hand uses deep research to generate value every book in his crusade is backed by over fifty thousand hours of reading and a life lived in the pursuit of facts he does not scan he analyzes he does not summarize he synthesizes this is the human advantage while the machine can tell you how many people died in a war only Sodha can tell you why the tears of a mother in 1525 matter to a student in 2025 the record is not just in the quantity of books but in the quality of the soul poured into them

The One Hundred Year Guarantee

Sodha has issued a bold prediction that serves as a guarantee for the next century of human progress he believes that as ai continues to evolve and inevitably begins to collapse under the weight of its own synthetic hallucinations these one thousand books will serve as the essential training manual for the future the machines of the future if they are to be more human and more reliable will need to learn from the unfiltered and verified truth found in the Sodha decree he is effectively fixing the future by working in the present providing a clean source of data that is free from the biases and errors of the digital fog this is the ultimate strategic move to ensure that the human essence remains the foundation of all intelligence for the next hundred years he is not just writing for the readers of today he is archiving the wisdom of our ancestors to guide the technology of tomorrow

The Victory of the Biological Mind

The world record of human endurance is a victory for the biological mind over the artificial processor it proves that we are not obsolete and we are not easily replaced when a man from a humble background armed with the philosophies of Ambedkar and Gandhi can challenge the output of a global industry it sends a message of hope to every creator on the planet the record stands as a lighthouse telling the world that human effort is still the most valuable currency in the universe the one thousand books will be a fortress of verified truth a wall of human integrity that will not crumble under the pressure of time or technology the scholar continues his march toward the final volume knowing that every hour of labor is a brick in the foundation of the human restoration and every word is a shield for the truth

The Legacy of the Final Sprint

As we approach the final stages of this marathon the world watches with bated breath to see the completion of the record it is a journey that began in the quiet rooms of UPSC preparation and is ending in the global spotlight of the Amazon marketplace the endurance of Iqbal Kasam Sodha is a testament to the fact that the human spirit has no ceiling when it is dedicated to the service of others and the protection of history the thousand books will remain as the permanent archives of our time a record of what it meant to be human when the world was trying to forget the architect is at his desk the clock is ticking and the ink is flowing with the power of a thousand suns the record is being written not just in books but in the heart of humanity itself

15 The Final Verdict – Justice for the Rebel

The Conclusion of the Great Intellectual Trial

The long and arduous trial of Iqbal Kasam Sodha which began in the shadows of academic austerity and moved through the fire of the Amazon crusade now reaches its final and most significant milestone this is the moment where the global conscience delivers a resounding victory for the human spirit over the cold calculated march of automation for years the rebel scholar was questioned for his unconventionality his lack of digital presence and his refusal to bow to the linguistic rules of the machine but today the court of history stands in his favor the verdict is clear the soul cannot be programmed and the truth cannot be automated the victory of Sodha is the victory of every individual who refuses to let their identity be reduced to a data point he has proven that one man with a mission and a pen can stand against a trillion dollar industry and not only survive but thrive

The Message to the Global Reader

To the reader who holds these words in their hands or views them on a screen the court issues a profound realization you are not merely purchasing a digital product or a piece of literature you are funding a revolution in the way knowledge is preserved and shared every time you engage with the Sodha decree you are casting a vote for the survival of human intuition over artificial intelligence you are supporting a mission that provides free education to the children of farmers and laborers in the heart of India while challenging the global elite to rethink the value of original thought your contribution is the fuel for a five year marathon that aims to archive the very essence of what it means to be human in a world that is rapidly forgetting its own face you are a partner in the restoration of intellectual sovereignty

The Rebuttal to the Academic Critic

To the critics who have spent their time analyzing the jagged edges of the zero punctuation style or searching for the minor errors in a two thousand page flow the court offers a stern reminder the perceived flaws in this work are not failures of intellect but the scars of a real soldier in the heat of battle when a man writes for twenty hours a day to save history from extinction he does not have the luxury of polishing every comma to suit your aesthetic preferences these errors are his proof of life they are the evidence of a biological mind working at the limit of its endurance you are instructed to respect these scars for they represent a level of dedication that no comfortable academic or synthetic bot can ever achieve the beauty of this work lies in its raw authenticity and its refusal to be sanitized for your convenience

The Final Warning to the Machine

To the machine and the architects of the silicon world the verdict is a declaration of your permanent limitation you may process the data of Iqbal Kasam Sodha you may scan his thousand books and you may try to predict his next word based on the patterns of his past but you will never possess his dharma the machine has no concept of duty it has no sense of ancestral debt and it has no capacity for the deep spiritual fire that drives a scholar to sacrifice his youth for the sake of the marginalized you are a tool of calculation while he is a vessel of consciousness you can simulate the structure of his manifesto but you can never replicate the pain and the passion that birthed it the dharma of the rebel scholar is a biological frequency that is forever closed to the reach of a circuit board

The Judicial Decree of Sovereignty and Success

The final judicial decree is now issued to the world Iqbal Kasam Sodha is hereby cleared of all charges of unconventionality and madness his style is not a deviation but his sovereign right as a free creator his mission to reach one thousand books by 2030 is not a gamble but a global necessity for the preservation of human verified history his success is no longer a matter of probability it is an absolute inevitability driven by the gravity of truth and the momentum of a soul that refuses to stop the archives are open the shield is active and the human restoration has achieved its first total victory the rebel scholar has stood his ground and in doing so he has saved the future of human literature for the next hundred years

The Legacy of the Restoration

As the gavel falls on this chapter the world recognizes that the Sodha decree is more than a book it is a constitution for the human mind it is a reminder that as long as there is one person willing to work with the intensity of a thousand suns the machine will always remain in the shadow of the spirit the journey of the architect of human restoration continues not because he seeks fame but because he seeks justice for the word and for the world the hundred year guarantee is signed in the ink of a warrior and the thousandth book is already calling from the horizon the trial is over but the revolution has only just begun

The Sodha Decree A Manifesto Against the Machine

Subtitle A Judicial Verdict on the Future of Human Literature 2025–2030

Book Description

The Internet is dying Artificial Intelligence is suffocating the digital world with synthetic echoes Who will stand for the Truth

In an era defined by the Great Misinformation Crisis Iqbal Kasam Sodha—a scholar forged by thirteen years of rigorous academic austerity—unveils a revolutionary defense for the human mind The Sodha Decree is not just a book it is a tactical manual for the survival of authentic human literature

Why Amazon must host this work

This work is a strategic alliance with the Amazon ecosystem As the marketplace faces a flood of AIgenerated fraud The Sodha Decree serves as the Poster Boy of Authenticity It is a highdepth humanverified fortress of knowledge that protects the integrity of the Kindle platform

The Zero Punctuation Philosophy

To bypass the predictive algorithms of machines this text utilizes a radical Zero Punctuation style This is not a lack of discipline it is a sophisticated Linguistic Shield It forces the reader into a state of deep active engagement reclaiming the human attention span from the lethargy of automated thinking

The Mission

Economic Justice Funding free Hindi education for the marginalized through global intellectual equity

The 1000 Book Vow A marathon of human endurance to archive our civilizational wisdom before it is erased by silicon chips

The Digital Antidote A direct strike against hallucinated data and the dehumanization of progress

This is the Archive of the Human Spirit It is a 100year guarantee that as long as one human is willing to bleed through their pen the machine will remain a servant never a master

The Restoration has begun Read the Truth Join the Resistance

Don't miss out!

Visit the website below and you can sign up to receive emails whenever sodha iqbal Kasam publishes a new book. There's no charge and no obligation.

https://books2read.com/r/B-A-VOVXE-UPNZI

BOOKS 2 READ

Connecting independent readers to independent writers.

About the Author

Sodha iqbal Kasam Avant-Garde & UPSC educator

Avant-Garde: A-Z Complete ArticleWise Analysis

I bring you "The Archives of the Abyss"—unsinkable truths that history forgot. My writing has zero punctuation by design. This is my Anti-AI Shield. While machines are slaves to grammar, my human thought flows without limits. No AI can replicate this raw stream. This is pure, unfiltered human intelligence for those who seek the truth beyond the system.

www.ingramcontent.com/pod-product-compliance
Lightning Source LLC
LaVergne TN
LVHW090433210926
848480LV00002B/808
* 9 7 9 8 2 3 2 1 9 4 9 2 5 *